the Space Merchants

ALR008

Published by

Aqualamb

The Space Merchants:
Carter Logan : Drums and Percussion
Aileen Brophy : Bass and Vox
Ani Monteleone : Vox and Keys
Michael Guggino : Vox and Guitars

One Cut Like the Moon, Evil Itch, Mainline the Sun, Beatniks engineered by
Aaron Bastinelli at Converse Rubber tracks , Williamsburg, Brooklyn July 2014.
Good Day to Die, Reavers, 1000 Years of Boredom, Where's the Rest of Life?
engineered by Josh Meakim at the Sex Dungeon in Philadelphia, PA May 2013.

Mixed by Michael Guggino
Mastered by Josh Bonati in Brooklyn, NY
Design by Braulio Amado
Photos by Andrew Strasser and Carter Logan

20 19 18 17 16 15 14 13 12 11 10 9 8 7 6 5 4 3 2 1 First edition

aqualamb.org

CONTENTS

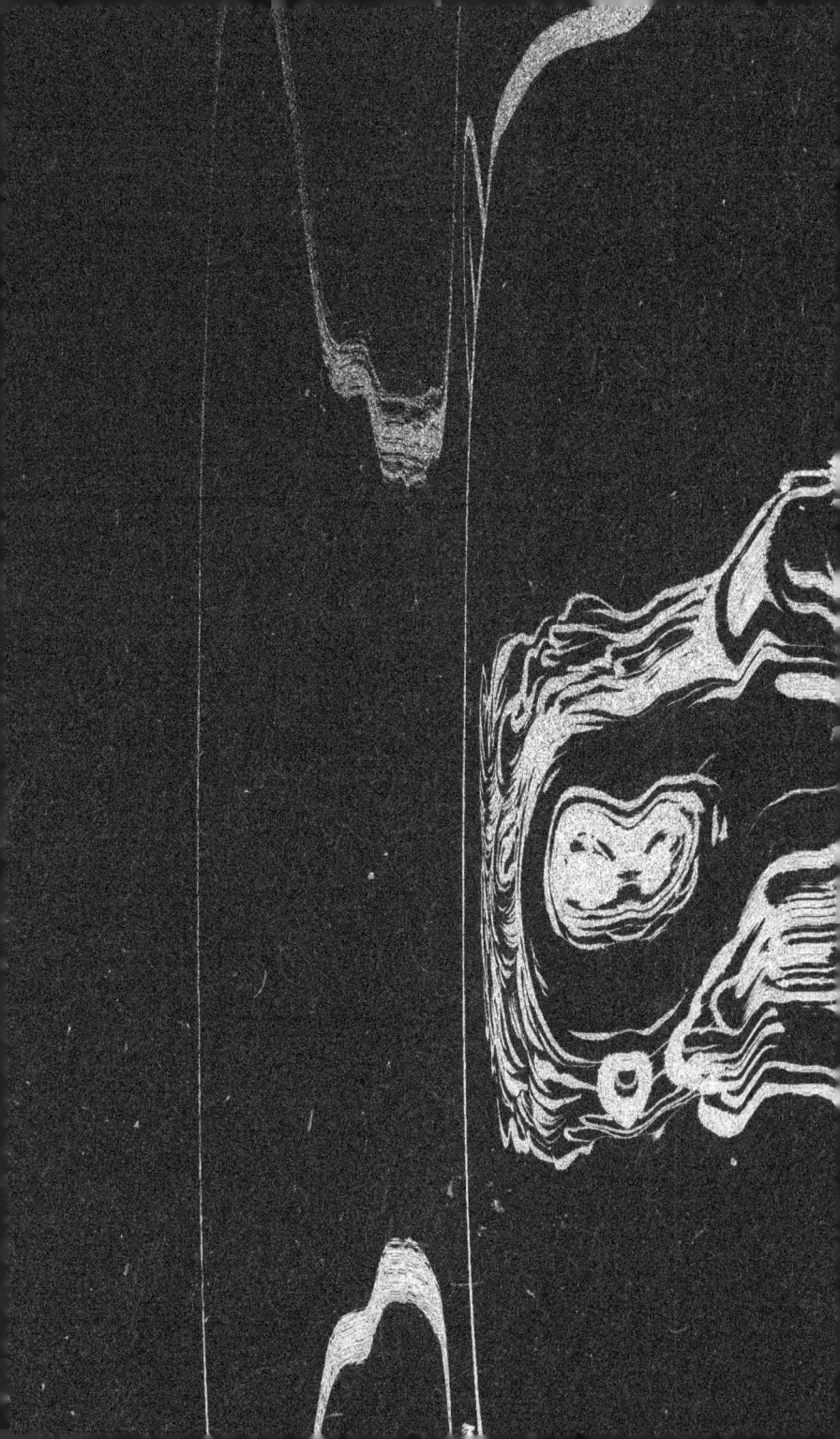

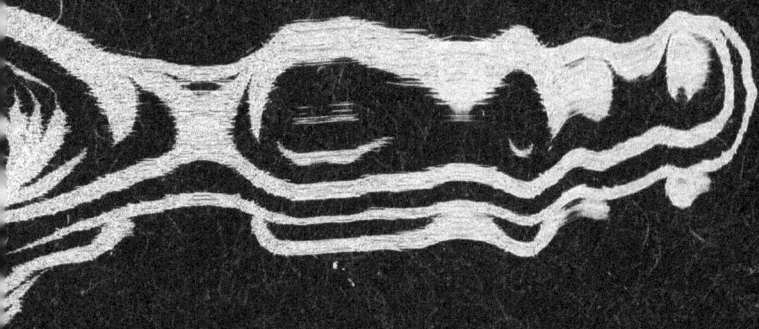

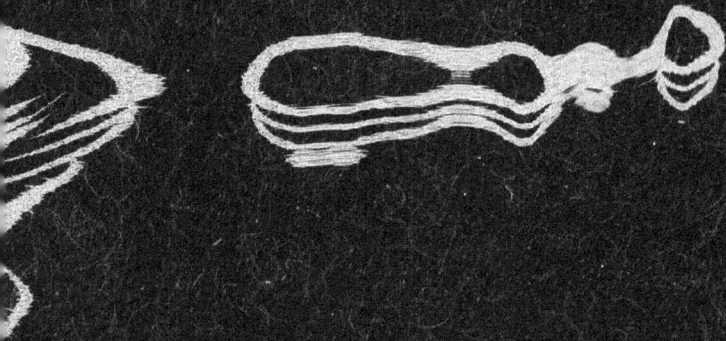

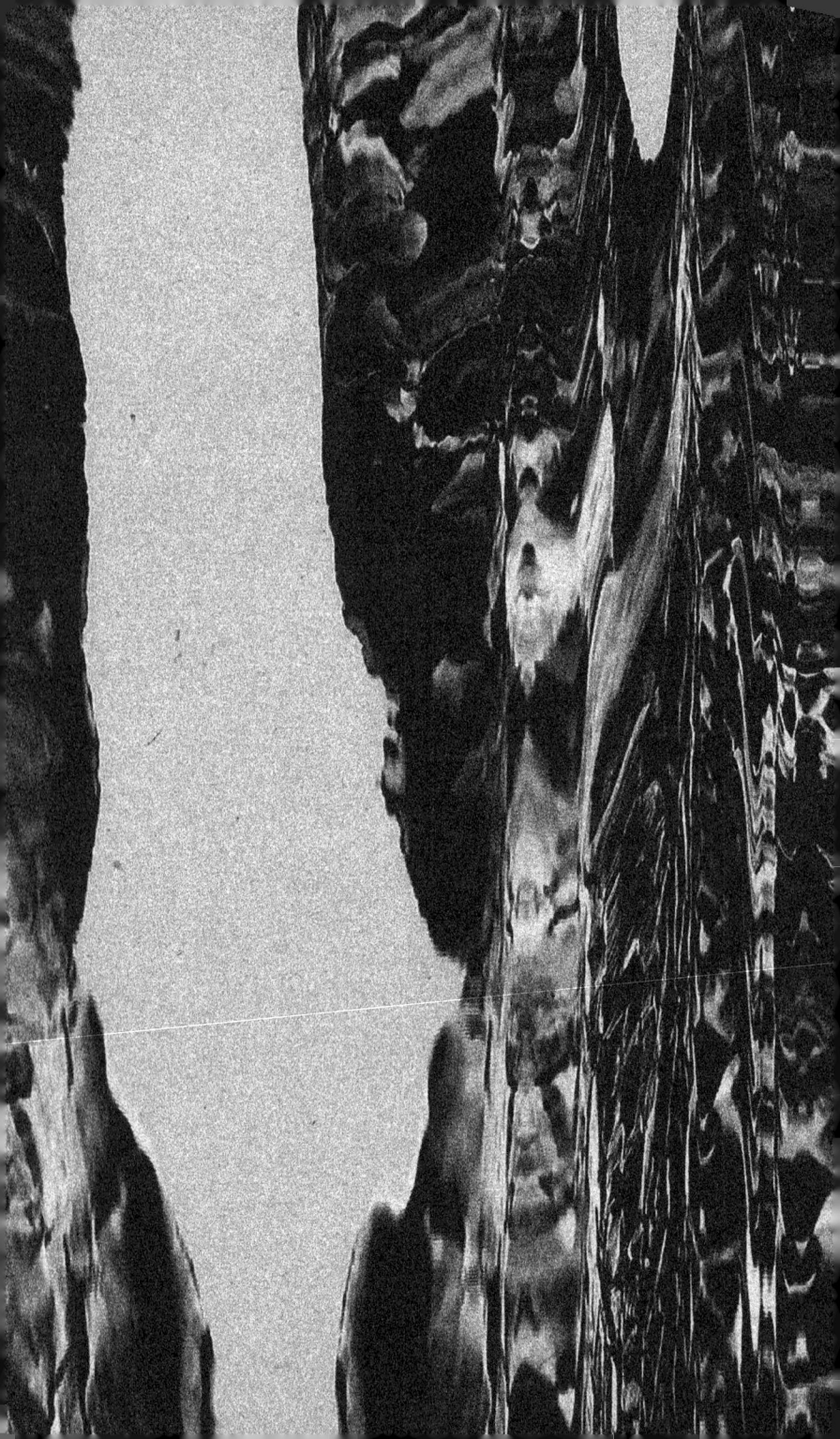

HUMAN SACRIFICE WAS A RELIGIOUS PRACTICE CHARACTERISTIC OF PRE-CO-
LUMBIAN AZTECS. IN THE AZTEC "LEGEND OF THE FIVE SUNS" ALL THE GODS
SACRIFICED THEMSELVES SO THAT MANKIND COULD LIVE. THEY BELIEVED ON
GOING SACRIFICE SUSTAINS THE UNIVERSE AND THAT ALL THINGS ON EARTH
GREW OUT OF THE SEVERED OR BURIED BODIES OF THE SACRIFICED GODS.

```
ONE          CUT          LIKE          THE          MOON




EVIL                    SPIRITS                    RISE
SO        SHARPEN          UP          YOUR        KNIFE
MAKE        ONE        CUT        LIKE        THE        MOON
DON'T    YOU    CRY    I'LL    BE    WITH    YOU    SOON
AT                    THE                    SACRIFICE
EVIL                    SPIRITS                    TALK
TIME        FOR        YOUR        EARLY        MORNING        WALK
MAKE        ONE        CUT        LIKE        THE        MOON
WHEN    I    SEE    MY    BLOOD    IT    MAKES    ME    SWOON
AT                    THE                    SACRIFICE
COME        TO        THE        SACRIFICE        AT        DAWN!
```

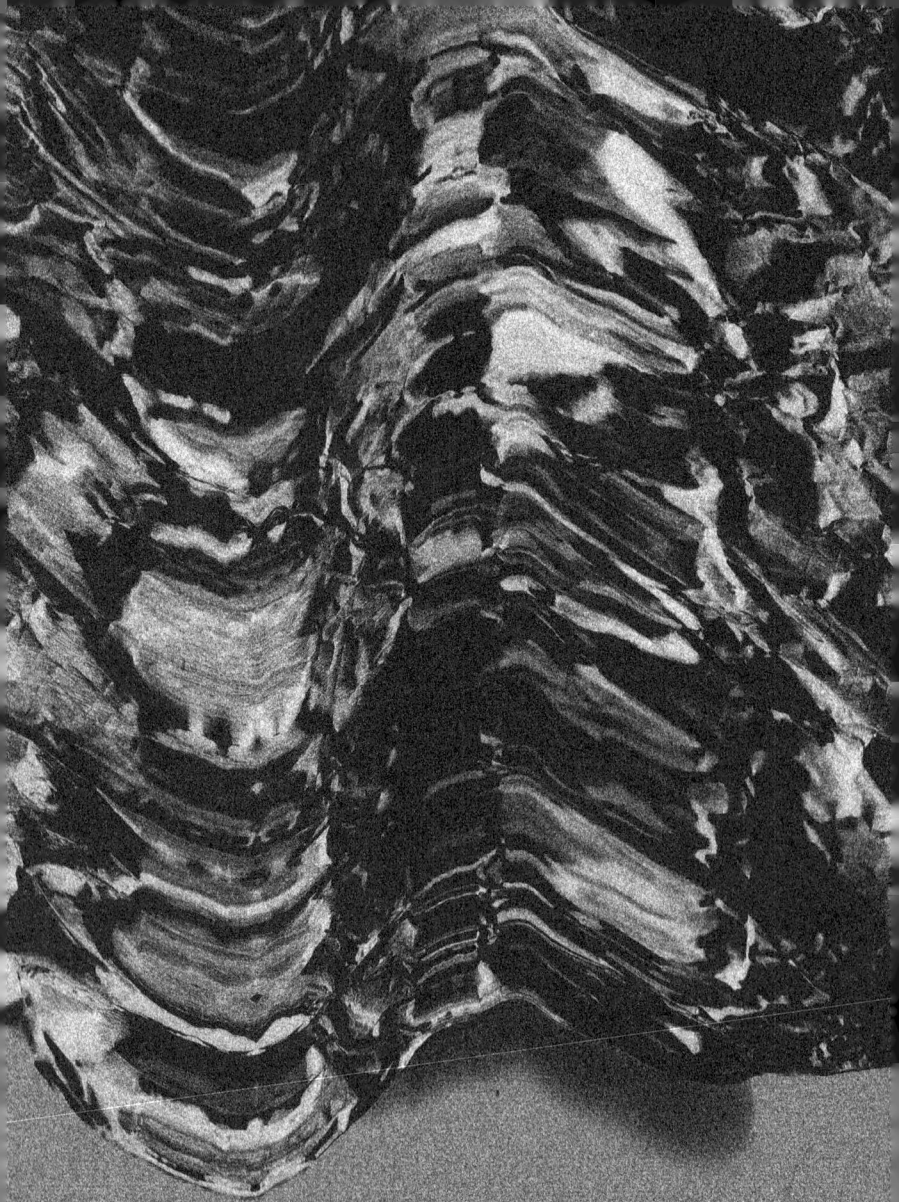

WE ALL KNOW THAT OUR TIME ON EARTH IS SHORT. DEATH IS ALWAYS LURKING

JUST OUT OF SIGHT. ENTROPY IS THE GRADUAL SLIDE OF ORDER INTO DISOR-

DER. IT'S THE WAY OF THE UNIVERSE. THE ONLY THING THAT DEFIES ENTROPY

IS LIFE. FOR A TIME, IT GROWS. BUT, IT EVENTUALLY MUST SUCCUMB.

THERE'S   A   MAN   IN   BLACK   COMING   FOR   MY   SOUL

HE   KNOWS   TOO   MANY   THINGS   I   DON'T   WANNA   KNOW

ALL   THE   GOOD   THINGS   I'VE   DONE   IN   MY   LIFE

HE   DON'T   WANNA   HEAR   IT,   MAN

WAITING   ALL   NIGHT   FOR   THE   MORNING   LIGHT

WAITING   FOR   THE   TIME   WHEN   THE   SUN   WILL   RISE

EVERYWHERE   I   GO,   I   CAN   FEEL   SOMEONE   NIPPING   AT   MY   TOES

CAN'T   TELL   IF   IT'S   COLD   OR   IT'S   JUST   YOUR   GHOST

PLEASE   LEAVE   ME   BE.

GIMME   ONE   CHANCE   TO   SAY   MY   GOODBYES

I'LL   BE   READY   TO   GO   WHEN   THE   SUN   RISE

THE EGYPTIAN BOOK OF THE DEAD EXPLAINED HOW TO NAVIGATE THE AF-
TERLIFE. THE INSTRUCTIONS WERE SPECIFIC AND COMPLICATED. HEAVEN
WAS THE MIDDLE OF THE DAY WHEN THE SUN WAS HIGH IN THE SKY. THAT
IS WHERE THEY WANTED TO SPEND ETERNITY. TO GET THERE THEY HAD TO
NAVIGATE A MAZE THAT LEADS THEM THROUGH EACH HOUR OF THE DAY UN-
TIL THEY REACHED THE PERFECT HOUR. EACH HOUR HAD A GATE THAT WAS
GUARDED BY A DEMON. IF THEY ANSWERED THE DEMONS' RIDDLES CORRECTLY
THEY WERE ALLOWED TO PROCEED UNTIL, FINALLY THEY MADE IT TO HEAVEN.

MAINLINE   THE   SUN   I   PUT   MY   WRIST   IN   THE   SKY

I'VE   BEEN   DOING   IT   FOR   YEARS   I'M   LIKE   EGYPTIAN

HOW'D   YOU   THINK   SHE   GOT   THAT   BODY   AND   HER   PERFECT   SKIN

EACH   HOUR   OF   THE   DAY   IS   A   ROOM   IN   THE   MAZE

MAINLINE   THE   SUN

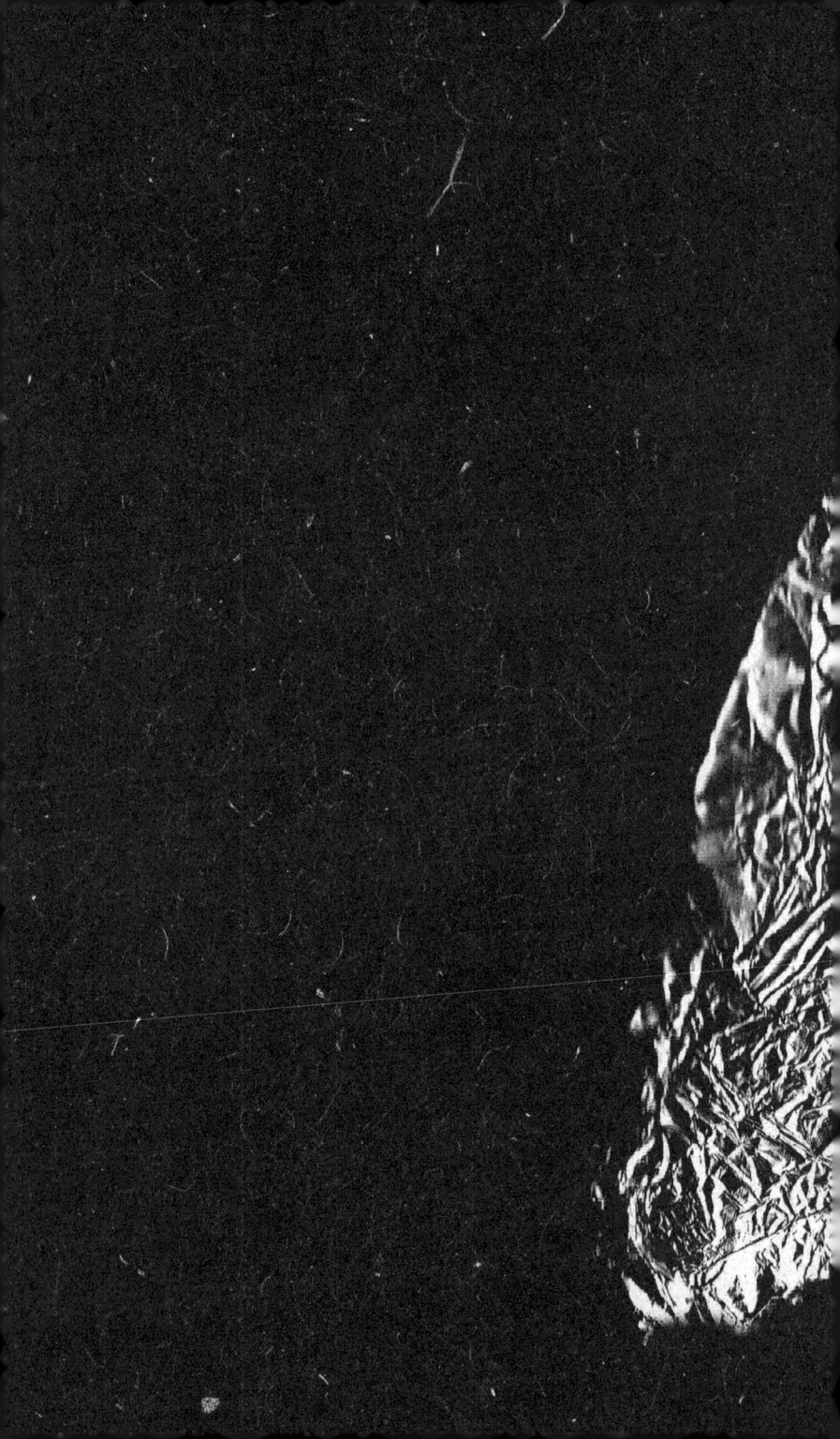

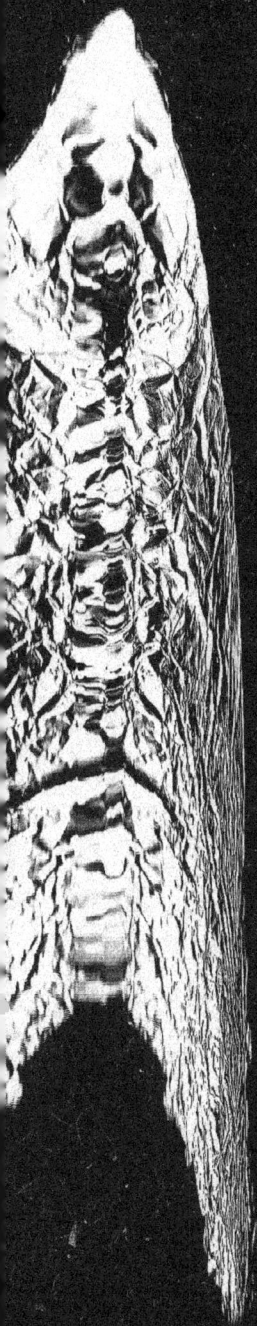

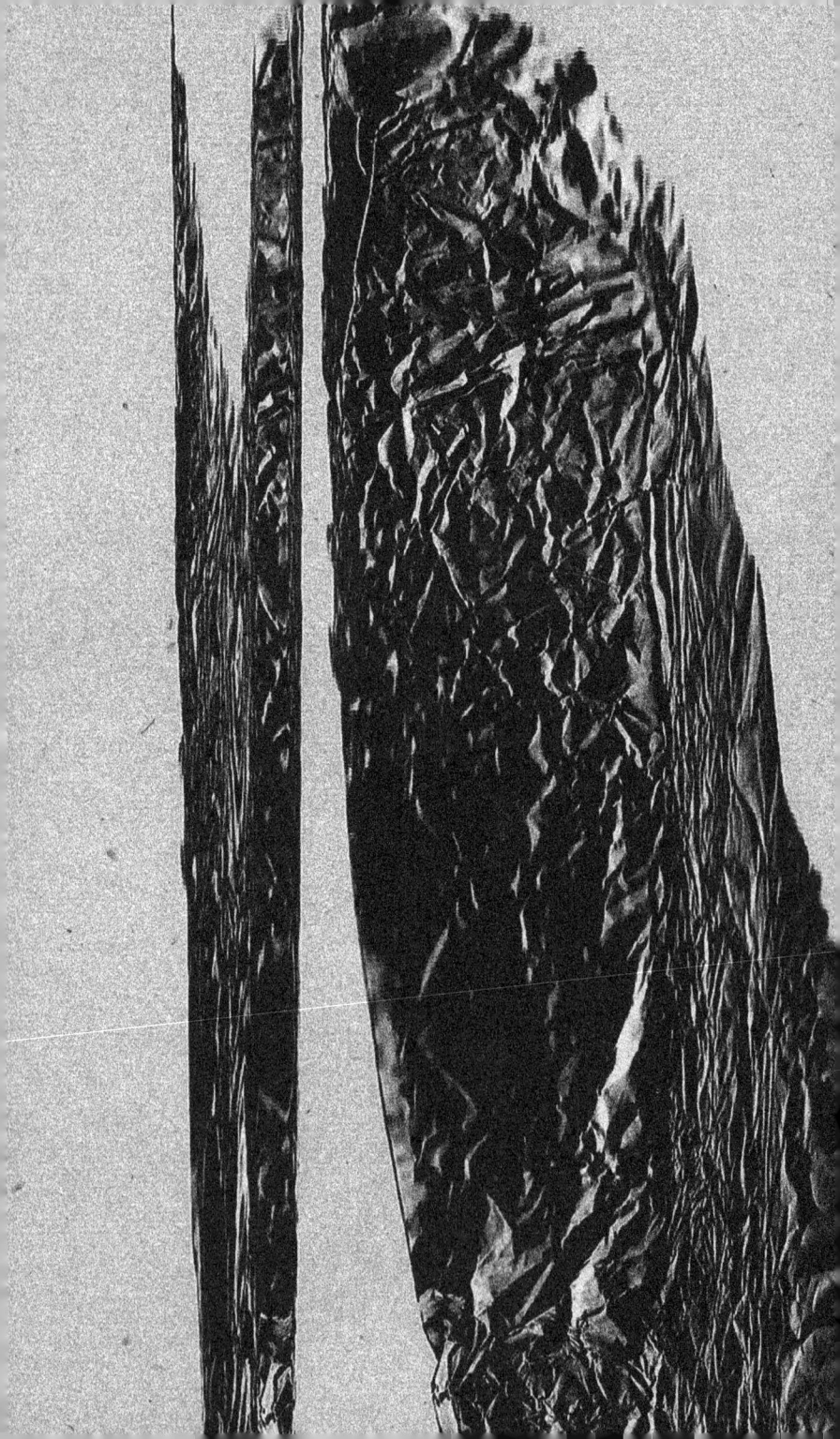

```
B       E       A       T       N       I       K       S


GET                                                     HIGH

STAY                                                    COOL

DON'T    LET    THEM    TELL    WHAT    YOU    CAN    DO

RELAX        AND       BABY        EASE        ON       IN

CAUSE   WHO   KNOWS   WHEN   WE'RE   GONNA   GET   TO   DO   THIS   AGAIN

WHAM            BABY            GOOD            GODDAMN
```

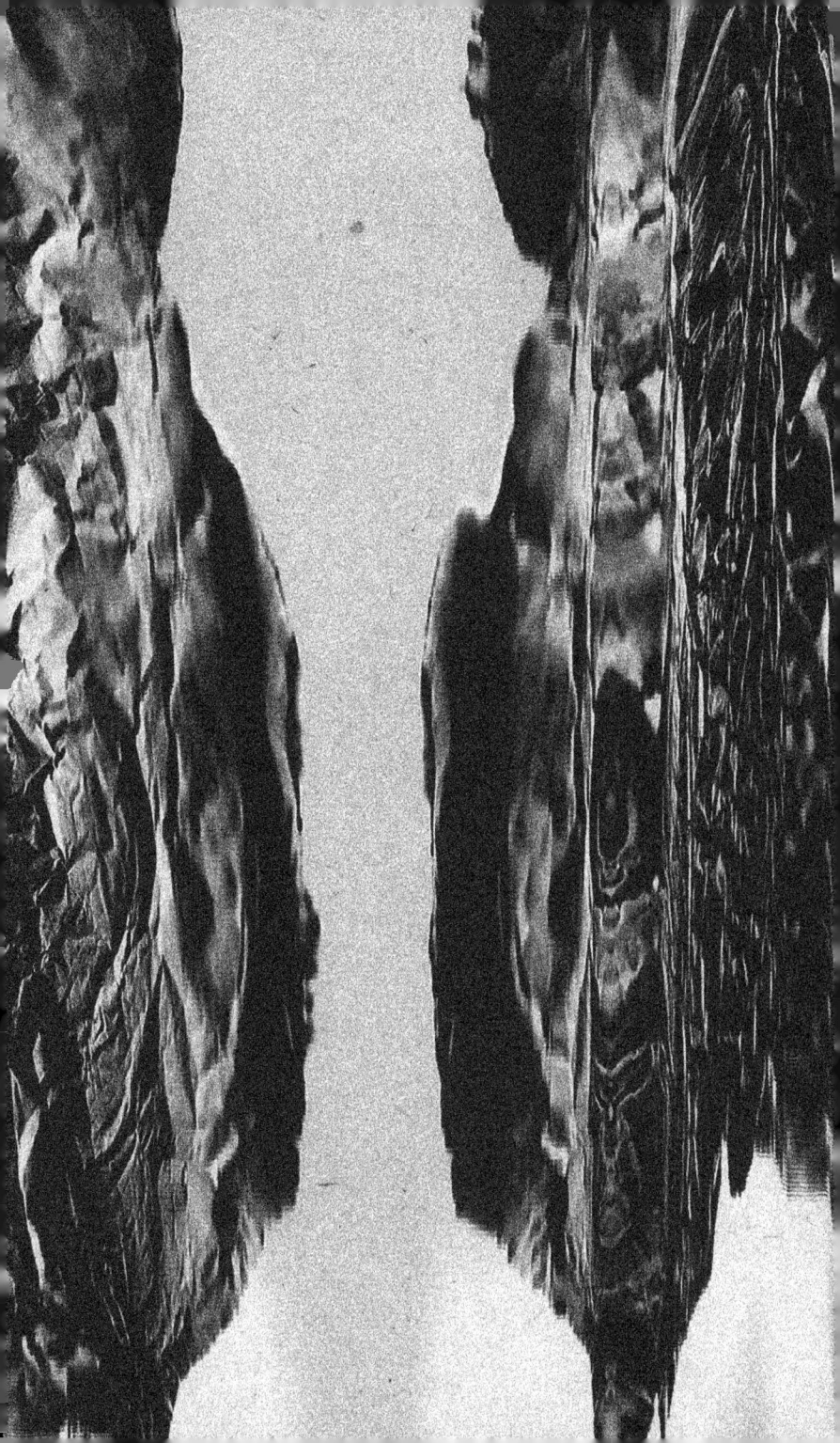

I GOT A CALL EARLY HALLOWEEN MORNING. IT WAS A CALL
I HOPED I'D NEVER GET. MY SISTER SAID IT WAS TIME. I
DROVE ALL NIGHT AND WATCHED THE SUNRISE OVER THE TURN-
PIKE, HOPING I WOULD GET THERE IN TIME TO SAY GOODBYE.

GOOD DAY TO DIE

BEHIND ME WAS A MOUNTAIN
AHEAD SOME KIND OF ROAD
MY STOMACH IT WAS CHURNING
COULDN'T BEAR A HEAVY LOAD
A MISTY COLORED PATH
MY TRIALS MAKE ME LAUGH
MY SKIN IS THICK WITH SWEAT
BUT I AIN'T FINISHED YET
AND NOTHIN'
NOTHIN' LASTS FOREVER
I SAT ON THE BED AND CRIED
PICK A GOOD DAY
CURL UP AND DIE
IF YOU COULD JUST HANG ON
TO THE RISING OF THE SUN
YOU'D SEE YOUR ONLY SONS
AND YOU COULD JUST PASS ON

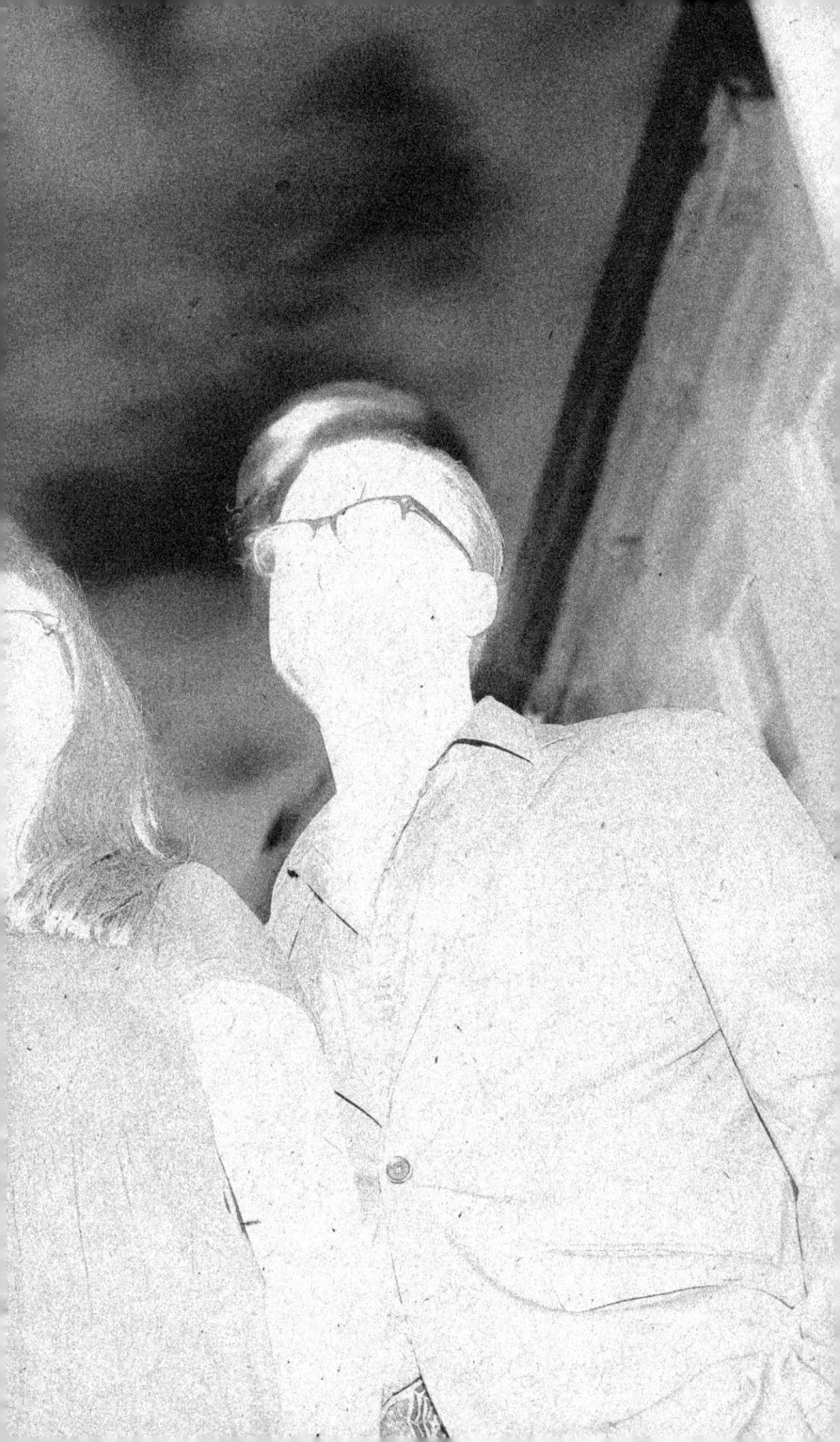

THEY SAID THERE WAS A GROUP OF MEN WHO WENT TO THE EDGE OF THE
UNIVERSE. WHEN THEY GAZED AT THE BLACKNESS IT SEEMED TO STRETCH
ON FOREVER. THE EXPANSE OF THE INFINITE VOID DROVE THEM MAD.
CURSED, THEY WANDER THROUGH SPACE, ENDLESSLY. IF YOU SHOULD EVER
COME ACROSS THESE MEN, TURN AND RUN. THEY ARE NOT YOUR FRIENDS.

IT'S   BEEN   FIFTEEN   YEARS   SINCE   I   STARTED   MY   ROUTE

I   KNOW   WHAT   THEY'LL   BE   TALKING   ABOUT

WHEN   I   SEE   TROUBLE   I   DON'T   PAY   IT   KNOW   MIND

WENT   TO   THE   EDGE   AND   I   LOST   MY   MIND

I   STARED   OUT   AT   IT   ALL

TAKE   ME   AWAY

I   STARED   OUT   AT   IT   ALL

LOCK   ME   UP   TAKE   ME   AWAY

IT   FEELS   LIKE   YOUR   DARK   MATTER   SET   ME   FREE.

GOD IS NOT A BEING, GOD IS BEING. ONE SUBSTANCE, MANY FORMS.

EVERY ATOM THAT MAKES UP THE WORLD AND OURSLEVES WAS FORGED IN

THE FURNACE OF A STAR. EACH ELEMENT CREATED FROM THE ASH OF

THE PREVIOUS ELEMENT. HYDROGEN BECOMES HELIUM BECOMES LITHIUM

UNTIL YOU GET TO HEAVIER ELEMENTS LIKE IRON AND GOLD. THESE

ELEMENTS TRAVELED ACROSS SPACE AND NOW THEY ARE YOU AND ME

AND EVERYTHING WE SEE. AFTER WE ARE ALL GONE THE ELEMENTS THAT

MADE US WILL STILL EXIST. TIME IS MEANINGLESS TO THEM. IN FACT

TIME IS ONLY IMPORTANT TO THE PARTICULAR COMBINATION OF ELE-

MENTS THAT CAME TOGETHER TO MAKE US CONSCIOUS. IN A WAY WE

LIVE FOREVER, BUT FOR MOST OF THAT TIME WE ARE UNAWARE OF IT.

1000   YEARS   OF   BOREDOM

ONE   THOUSAND   YEARS   OF   BOREDOM
CULMINATES   TODAY
MY   FEAR   IT   IS   NOT   WITH   ME
I   UP   AND   RAN   AWAY
GAZE   OUT   UPON   THE   STARLIGHT
ITS   LAUGHTER   ECHOES   ON

THE   SUN   WILL   COME   AGAIN
IT   MIGHT   NOT   COME   AGAIN

ONE   MILLION   YEARS   OF   ANGER
THE   FIRES   RAGE   TODAY
SMOKE   BLACK   UNFORGIVING
RIGHTS   WHERE   SUNLIGHT   MEETS   THE   SEA
I   WISH   WE   COULD   FORGIVE   THEM
BUT   I   KNOW   THEY'LL   NEVER   SEE

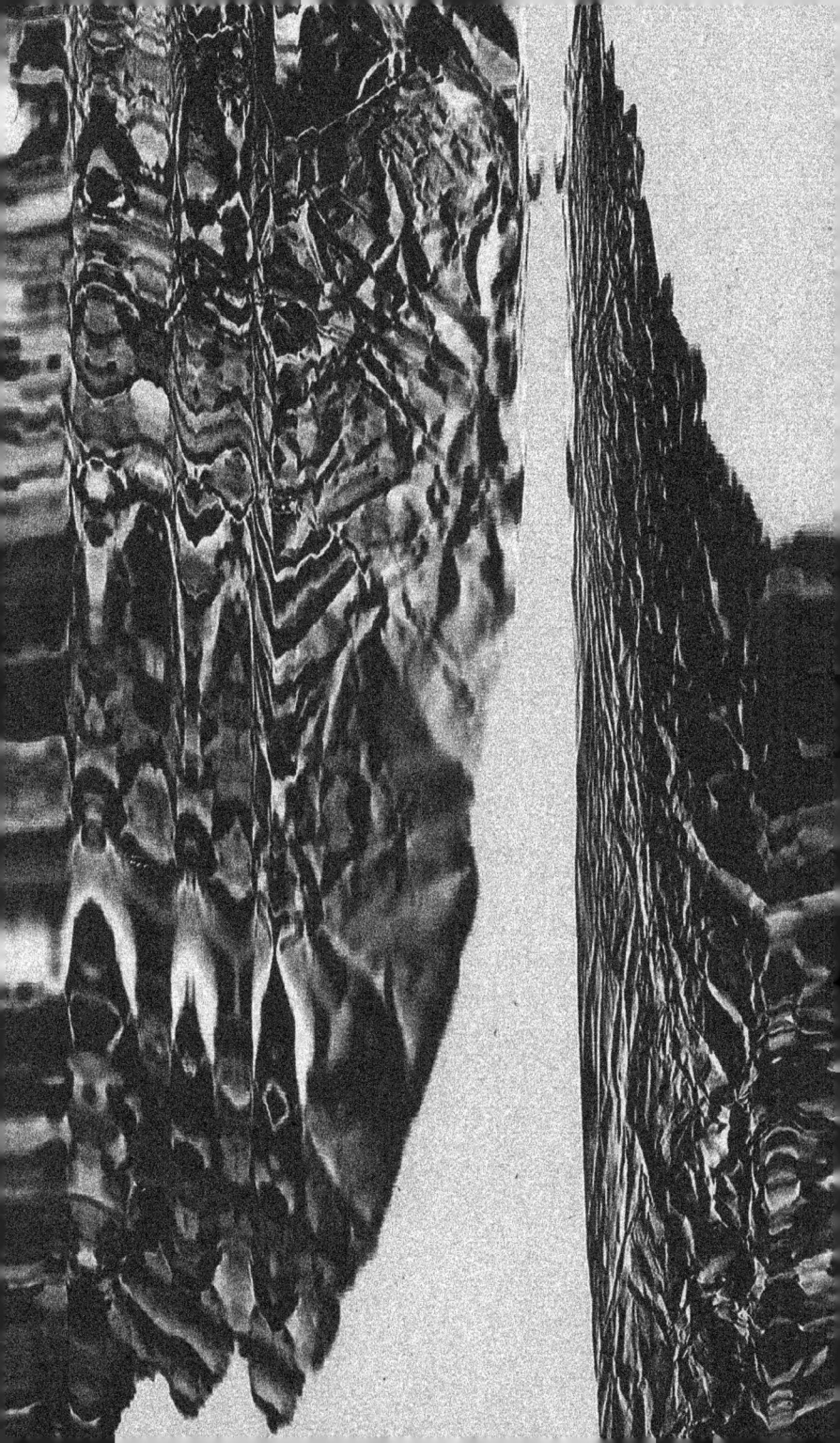

THE ODDS OF LIFE ON OTHER WORLDS, SOMEWHERE IN THE UNIVERSE, ARE HIGH. THERE ARE BILLIONS OF STARS AND EVEN MORE PLANETS AND EVEN MORE MOONS. SOMEWHERE OUT THERE MUST BE SOMETHING. RIGHT? MAYBE THERE ARE TINY CREATURES FLOATING IN A PRIMORDIAL STEW NEAR A RED OR YELLOW SUN OR GIANT BEASTS GRAZING ON PLAINS OF GRASS ON SOME LUSH MOON. IF YOU THINK ABOUT IT, WE REALLY HAVEN'T BEEN LOOKING FOR THAT LONG. NOT EVEN A BLINK IN THE COSMIC EYE. PLANETS AND STARS HAVE COME AND GONE. CIVILIZATIONS COULD HAVE RISEN AND FALLEN. YET, WE WILL NEVER KNOW. MAYBE WE WILL GET A POSTHUMOUS MESSAGE FROM SOMEONE ON A PLANET THAT DOESN'T EXIST ANYMORE. THE VOICE OF A GHOST HURDLING THROUGH SPACE JUST BEGGING TO BE HEARD. UNTIL THEN, WE WILL SEARCH. BUT I WANT TO KNOW, WHERE'S THE REST OF LIFE?

WHERE'S   THE   REST   OF   LIFE?

SAID   ALL   MY   PRAYERS   IN   THE   BEDROOM
TRY   TO   SLEEP   REAL   WELL   AT   NIGHT
BEEN   TO   THE   STARS   AND   THE   PLANETS
YOU   THINK   THAT   KEEPS   ME   WARM   AT   NIGHT
SPACE   IS   REAL   COLD   AND   THE   VACCUM   THERE
SURE   TO   TAKE   YOUR   BREATH   AWAY
WHEN I'M HOME I THINK ABOUT IT SOMETIMES YEAH IT REALLY TAKES ME AWAY
WHERE'S   THE   REST   OF   LIFE
SAID   ALL   MY   PRAYERS   IN   THE   BEDROOM
YEAH   I   SLEEP   REAL   WELL   AT   NIGHT
BEEN   TO   THE   STARS   AND   THE   GALAXIES   UP   THERE
YOU   THINK   IT   KEEPS   ME   WARM   AT   NIGHT
ROCKET   SHIPS   ARE   COLD   AND   LONESOME   YOU   SAY
YEAH   YOU'D   BE   RIGHT
WHEN I'M HOME I THINK ABOUT IT SOMETIMES YEAH IT REALLY TAKES ME AWAY
WHERE'S   THE   REST   OF   LIFE
COMING   DOWN   BABY   YEAH   I   HIT   THE   PLANET   SIDE
COMING   DOWN   FAST   AND   ALL   I   SEE   IS   PARACHUTE   WHITE
I   FEEL   ALL   RIGHT

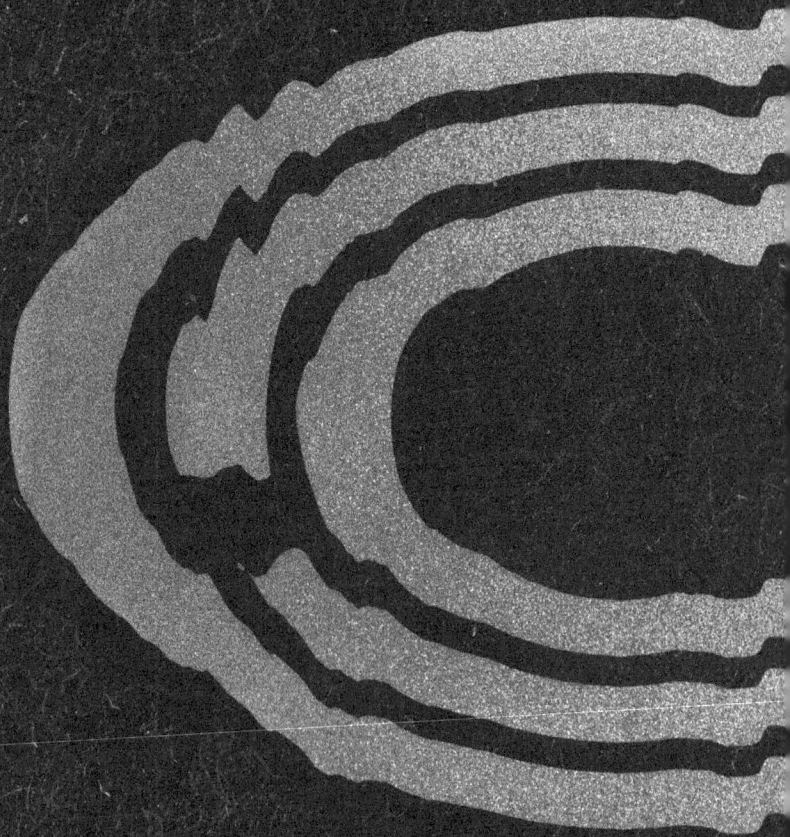

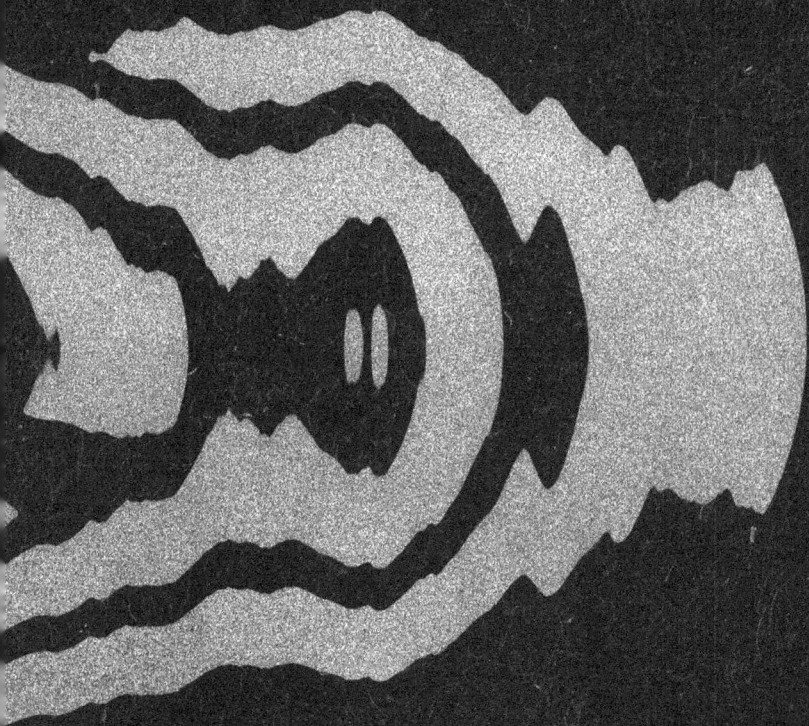

the
SPACE
MERCHANTS

The music for this release can be downloaded
via the link below:

http://aqualamb.org/008

Aqualamb

AVAILABLE FROM AQUALAMB ARTISTS

☐ **DESCENDER by Descender** (ALR 001)
6 song debut EP. Available formats: Digipak CD, digital download, streaming
90's Influenced Post-Hardcore. RIYL: Snapcase, Helmet, Quicksand

☐ **AND SO WE MARCHED by Descender** (ALR 002)
4 song EP. Available formats: Printed book, digital download, streaming
90's Influenced Post-Hardcore. RIYL: Snapcase, Helmet, Quicksand

☐ **TAKING DRUGS TO MAKE MUSIC TO SELL CARS TO** (ALR 003)
by Human Highlight Reel
4 song debut EP. Available formats: Vinyl record, printed book, digital download, streaming
Instrumental Post Rock. RIYL: Maserati, June of 44, Russian Circles

☐ **JUDGE by Vagina Panther** (ALR 004)
5 song EP. Available formats: Printed book, digital download, streaming
Heavy Female Fronted Garage Rock. RIYL: QOTSA, Cheeseburger, Fu Manchu, Stooges

☐ **BLACK BLACK BLACK by Black Black Black** (ALR 005)
12 song debut LP. Available formats: Vinyl record, printed book, digital download, streaming
Melodic Death Rock. RIYL: Akimbo, Torche, Lungfish, Black Flag

☐ **GODMAKER by Godmaker** (ALR 007)
4 song debut LP. Available formats: Printed book, digital download, streaming
Doomy Sludge Metal. RIYL: High on Fire, Red Fang, Mastodon, The Sword

☐ **SPACE MERCHANTS by Space Merchants** (ALR 008)
8 song debut LP. Available formats: Printed book, digital download, streaming
Whiskey-soaked Space Rock. RIYL: Black Mountain, Black Angels, Dead Meadow, The Besnard Lakes

☐ **HIRAM-MAXIM by Hiram-Maxim** (ALR 009)
4 song debut LP. Available formats: Vinyl record, printed book, digital download, streaming
Noisy Experimental Doomgaze. RIYL: Swans, Suicide, Pink Floyd, Oxbow

COMING SPRING 2015

☐ **LIGHTS DOWN / SHORT BREATHS by Descender** (ALR 010)
2 song single. Available formats: 7" vinyl, digital download, streaming
90's Influenced Post-Hardcore. RIYL: Snapcase, Helmet, Quicksand

All releases are available online at aqualamb.org

www.ingramcontent.com/pod-product-compliance
Lightning Source LLC
Chambersburg PA
CBHW051735040426
42447CB00008B/1137